Benedi at Saratoga

by Emma Nelson

illustrated by Rick Whipple

HOUGHTON MIFFLIN

BOSTON

The first time I saw Benedict Arnold, he was striding past our tent in his blue uniform. He walked with a slight limp, a souvenir from his campaign in Canada, when a musket ball had shattered his left leg. The way he carried himself was as if he was defying someone to stop him. My Pa had admired him and so I did, too. Pa often told me stories about Benedict Arnold, and how he had been responsible for preventing the British invasion of America in 1776. These were heroic stories. With only a small navy gathered in Canada, Arnold held off the British until the harsh winter set in. It was said that Arnold was responsible for keeping the British from conquering America.

I often wondered how Benedict Arnold became the man he was. Maybe he started out as a boy like me. But Pa told me some curious things. Arnold's great-grandfather was the first governor of Rhode Island. So you'd think he was destined straight for politics. Instead, he left school when he was thirteen, and roamed the streets. I guess he liked his independence. And Pa said he must have had some kind of smarts to survive on the streets. But Arnold also landed in trouble on a regular basis. So his family apprenticed him to Dr. Daniel Lathrop, his mother's cousin, who ran an apothecary. Pa said he learned a lot there, like how to prepare medicines—and other things, from horse care to music to accounting.

Can you believe that, with all these advantages, Arnold ran away twice—to fight in the French and Indian War! Still, when he turned eighteen, Dr. Lathrop asked him to be his chief clerk. A few years later, Arnold decided to use the money that Dr. Lathrop had given him to open his own apothecary shop in New Haven. Pa said he was so successful that by the time he was twenty-six, Arnold owned three ships and many horses, which he traded for sugar and cotton in the Caribbean. Arnold knew that the British had placed trade limitations on America. But he saw this as a business opportunity, which he took advantage of by smuggling rum, sugar, and molasses. This made him huge profits.

Watching him stride by that first time, I thought I understood the determination in his posture, and the haughtiness in the upward tilt of his chin. Despite his success in business, when Arnold tried to enter politics, he was snubbed by the New Haven aristocracy, who saw him as a crude outsider. This stung him bitterly, Pa said, and made him more ruthlessly independent.

I saw him again two weeks later. He was a man I'd feared—and for good reason. First, there were Pa's stories. Then there was the actual sight of him—tall, powerful, proud—and intimidating.

But that day in the soldiers' graveyard changed my mind. At first, I didn't even see him. My mind tumbled with the wind that blew swirls of dirt across Pa's grave, and my heart was lost. I was staring speechless at the inscription on Pa's marker when I felt a hand on my shoulder.

"Your father was our best scout. You loved him, didn't you?" General Arnold said.

As we stood in the graveyard, I couldn't believe it was Arnold. His sympathy seemed genuine. He felt so sorry about Pa's death that he made me his batman—his servant. That meant that I could still eat. When a soldier is killed, his relatives don't get fed; they must leave camp, even if they are only thirteen, like me. But General Arnold wouldn't let me leave.

"Wait till we thrash Gentleman Johnny," Arnold said. "Then it'll be safe to go home to New Hampshire."

"Gentleman Johnny" was General John Burgoyne, the British commander. He and five thousand Redcoats were camped four miles north of our position in Saratoga, New York. Burgoyne was eager to march south along the Hudson River so that he could trap General George Washington's army. It was our job to block him. Washington and Arnold were great friends, and though most in government resented Arnold as a nuisance, Washington always defended him.

Being a batman wasn't difficult; all I had to do was stick close to the General and follow orders. I polished his boots and saddled up his horse, Mercy. I brought him food, carried his messages, and cleaned his tent.

On September 19, 1777, I even went with him to battle. At around ten o'clock that morning, our scouts spotted 2,000 Redcoats. Quickly, the drummers beat out the signal that meant "To arms!" Men hurriedly grabbed muskets, lead shot, and powder horns, then ran to their places behind our redoubt, a half-mile long dirt barricade on Bemis Heights.

Atop this high bluff, you could see for miles. To the north was Freeman's Farm, a clearing carved out of the forest. Somewhere nearby the British were arming for battle.

General Arnold stared at the clearing, and I could tell he was itching to send our troops down there. It upset him when he couldn't do things his way. His superior officer, General Horatio Gates, who headed the American army at Saratoga, wanted the enemy to come to him. So we were forced to sit behind the redoubt on Bemis Heights. It was obvious that Arnold and Gates disliked each other. Arnold scowled as he told me how General Gates always took credit for Arnold's victories.

General Arnold stood quietly, as if formulating a plan. He looked north toward Freeman's Farm. Then he called my name.

"Ephraim, come with me," he said, stalking off toward General Gates's hut. He left me outside while he went in. I heard him say, in a tone that brooked no questions, that our boys did their best fighting hidden behind trees, rocks, and stone walls. They could win the battle.

As I peered through a window, I saw that General Gates looked like he'd just swallowed vinegar. But he gave in. So when the Redcoats came out of the woods on the north side of Freeman's Farm, our men were waiting for them on the south side—and the battle was on.

When the fight erupted, General Arnold and I were galloping toward Freeman's Farm. I couldn't see over the General's shoulder, but from the explosions of muskets and cannons, I could tell we were heading toward the worst of it. I broke out in a sweat. Then we passed some dead soldiers in a ditch. I screamed, thinking of my Pa, and the General pulled his horse to a stop.

"Go back there, boy," he said. "Climb up that big maple and stay put." Then he was off. From the safety of the tree, I looked down on the battle and watched thousands of men try to kill one another. I imagined this was what Pa went through before he was killed. I didn't like the idea of Redcoats swinging their bayonets at my father. But maybe he had entered battle like Arnold: brave, without fear or reservation.

Witnessing the battle cured me of the thought that war was glorious. Men were dying in agony, and all I could do was helplessly watch. But General Arnold amazed me. He was all over the place, pointing his sword first at one target, then at another. The more he risked his life, the more our men risked theirs. After an hour, the British fell back, and gradually, the shooting stopped.

At mid-afternoon, the General led a surprise attack on the Redcoats. He showed more energy than fifty soldiers, but it wasn't enough. At dusk, fresh German troops who fought for the British charged onto the field shouting and shooting. The Continentals—our men—were too tired to resist. They retreated into the darkness, and the carnage stopped. About 900 men were killed or wounded that day, nearly a third of them ours.

That battle was followed by a tense standoff that lasted for more than two weeks. We knew the British would try to fight their way past us, but we didn't know when. Then one day, when the officers were at lunch, a scout dashed in, reporting that Burgoyne had prepared his troops for battle. General Gates ordered a few hundred men to go see what was going on. Immediately Arnold stood, shouting that this wasn't enough, and that Gates had to send forth a stronger force. But Gates quickly cut Arnold off and ordered him to stay clear of the fight.

So the battle began without General Arnold. For maybe thirty minutes, he paced back and forth in his tent, listening impatiently to the *pop-pop-pop* of muskets in the distance. Finally, he could take no more. Barking at me to saddle Mercy, he said that we were going to battle. All the men we passed on the way to Freeman's Farm cheered us as we rode by, for they knew that Arnold was a strong, battle-hardened leader.

Hearing a call from behind us, I turned and saw a major from General Gates's staff, approaching us fast. Gates meant to capture us and take us back.

But Arnold simply dug his spurs into Mercy, and in a cloud of dust, we left the major behind. General Arnold found another tree for me to hide in, pulled out his sword, and galloped away. He yelled at the soldiers and rallied them to the fight.

I couldn't take my eyes off the General. At one point,
he ran Mercy through a gauntlet of American and British
soldiers who were firing at each other! I held my breath, but
the General wasn't even grazed.

Since the last battle, the Redcoats had built two small
barricades. The General led a charge against one, then
wheeled around and led 300 men against the other.

In a couple of minutes, dozens of wounded and dead
German defenders were sprawled all over the ground.
Suddenly I saw one of them moving—and he was aiming his
musket at the General.

Arnold shuddered in his saddle, seizing his leg with both hands. He was hit, his right thigh shattered. Another musket ball ripped into Mercy's head. The horse reared up and collapsed on the General's wounded leg. For a moment, I watched in disbelief. Then I jumped down from my tree and sprinted across the field, swept along by a gale of grief and anger.

We made a stretcher for General Arnold out of two poles and a blanket. As soldiers carried him away, he looked up at me and told me it was safe to return home. As I walked away I heard him mutter, "I wish it had been my heart."

That same day, Gentleman Johnny surrendered to General Gates, and the Battle of Saratoga officially ended. Thanks to General Arnold, the Continentals had kept the British from trapping General Washington. And they had proven that they could beat one of the world's best armies. I sure wish Pa had been there to see it.

Postscript

Though this story is partly fictional, it tells about real events. Benedict Arnold was a real figure, and he led the Patriot forces to victory in the fighting at Saratoga. He was badly wounded in that battle, as well as in earlier fighting. In the first years of the war, many people considered Benedict Arnold to be the best and bravest general on the American side.

Yet few people today remember Benedict Arnold for his bravery and leadership. Those who remember him at all recall his treachery. In 1780, Arnold switched sides, joining the British. He was offered 20,000 pounds, about the equivalent of one million dollars today. Yet he only collected about a third of this money.

Arnold became a ranking general of the Loyalist troops—Americans who supported British rule. He betrayed his friend George Washington, who was devastated by Arnold's defection. When the revolution was over, Arnold lived in exile in England for the rest of his life. He was unhappy in his new home. Everyone knew of his treachery, and even the British no longer trusted him. He died poor and alone.

Why *did* Arnold betray his country? No one knows for sure. He may have acted for the money, or for a higher position in the opposing army. Another factor might have been his habitual mistreatment by the American government and those in power who saw him as a threat and an inferior.

Perhaps Arnold was disillusioned after all those years spent fighting for a country that didn't seem to like or respect him. In any case, treasonous or not, he would always have been an outsider in his own country.

The name Benedict Arnold has become synonymous with betrayal and treason. Still, it is worth remembering that the American cause might never have survived, had it not been for Arnold's heroics at Saratoga.